Driving Through Life
What Was I Thinking?

A Guide to Hope
After an Autism Diagnosis

Thomas Burton

Abundant
LIFE
PUBLICATIONS

ISBN-Paperback Edition: 978-1-956184-02-0

Printed in the United States of America

Published by: Abundant Life Publications LLC

Edited by: SLT Inspirations LLC

Dedication

I dedicate this book to my parents.

I am thankful for my parents.

I am thankful that my Father was present to help me

through the difficult stages of my life.

Thanks to my Lord and Savior Jesus Christ for giving me

the opportunity to write this book.

Thanks to my family and daughters for their

prayers and support.

Thanks to my pastor and church family.

Thanks to my life coach.

Thanks to all who have taken time to invest in this book

and read it.

Table of Contents

Chapter 1: Page 10

Childhood Years and Growing Pains

Chapter 2: Page 22

Love and Marriage

Chapter 3: Page 26

Diagnosis

Chapter 4: Page 38

 Renewed Mindset

Chapter 5: Page 48

On the Right Path

Chapter 6: Page 54

Faith Forward

Chapter 7: Page 62

Resources

Prologue

A poem that I wrote during my journey with autism.

Been living on the spectrum all these years.

Many tears and fears,

I did not know what was wrong,

I started singing a sad song.

Many issues, I went for help, I was told nothing was wrong.

Wondering in the wilderness as the children of Israel,

but did not know what was wrong.

Years later, I was diagnosed on the spectrum.

On the spectrum, cost my family relationships and it has

taken a toll on my soul.

Started to ask the question,

"If God is with us, why is all of this befallen us?"

So many questions, so much frustration, God please help

me as I continue this journey in life.

You are driving, taking a road trip on the interstate,

it's a nice clear sunny day.

You drive a few miles down the road and encounter a

thunderstorm that was not forecast.

This storm is intense with thunder,

lightning and heavy rains to the point you have to pull over

and wait for the rain to stop.

We pray when we get in our cars we would arrive safely

where we are going.

Just like the storm mentioned in this poem,

sometimes life can be unpredictable.

CHAPTER

1

Childhood Years
and
Growing Pains

I was born the third oldest of seven children. My parents told me that I was born premature and as a result, I remained at the hospital several days. Being the middle child was difficult for me because the youngest children and the oldest children received the most attention.

As a result, I thought people were not paying any attention to me. When it came to my parents, I felt left out. At one point in life, I had to take on a leadership role when one of my siblings was diagnosed early on with a developmental delay.

My family is very musically inclined. My father played the piano and organ, and my mother was a singer. In fact, at one time we had a gospel music family singing group. Music has always been a big part of my life. I often invested a lot of time into listening to music of many different genres.

Gospel music is my favorite genre because it tells the story about God helping people get through difficult times in life. I enjoy playing the bass guitar and I tried singing from time to time. When I practice my music, that serves as another form of healing for me.

When I practice my music, I feel closer to God. In my opinion, worship is a peaceful time between me and God. When I add music during my time of worship, it is still a peaceful experience. In my opinion, praise is more vocal and has more sound.

For me, music was a form of therapy. I believe music helped me to stay focused as a child. I would get in the car and listen to music. Some of my childhood highlights include receiving toys at Christmas and listening to music. At Christmas, me and one of my brothers talked about sports and watched games together.

We often fell asleep by the second game of the day after our good meal had digested. I also enjoyed watching television programs with music during the holiday season.

As a child, I pursued piano lessons and I've sang with choirs. I also like the acoustic guitar because the sound is soothing to me. I recently read a report that music therapy helps people with autism.

Sharing was instilled in me at an early age. My mother was an only child and my father was not an only child. There was a visible difference in the way my parents shared. My father was mostly responsible for the discipline.

I experienced some joy during my childhood, but I also experienced some traumatic growing pains as a child. I was sexually abused at an early age by a relative. When I started grade school, I was a very quiet child.

Some people considered me to be a loner; however, I was actually somewhat afraid of people because of the sexual abuse. Being alone was a way to protect myself from people. I was always somewhat shy, but the sexual abuse made it even worse. Sometimes people were offended because I didn't talk that much. After school, I went to my room and remained quiet.

When I was in school, I did not talk to other children. Some children were okay with my quietness; however, other children often asked, "What's wrong with you?" Some of the children did their homework together in school. However, I did not. I took my homework home and completed my homework by myself. The experience of sexual abuse caused me to be more of an introvert. The children found out that I had been abused, so I had a difficult time protecting myself from other children. It got to the point that children started jumping on me at school.

I had problems protecting myself in school from bullies. This was a problem I could not seem to solve. One time in middle school, another child wanted to fight me for no reason. That child also had a weapon and planned to use it on me, but God protected me. After that incident, I was convinced that school was not for me. I told my parents I would drop out and attend a GED program. God came to my rescue again when we moved out of that school district.

I started ninth grade at a new school and I did not have any problems with school bullies. However, I was very withdrawn and did not talk to anyone. I visited a school counselor once after the sexual abuse; however, it was not helpful for me at that time. I believe the lack of consistent counseling concerning the sexual abuse as a child caused me to be more withdrawn from people. My academics were okay, but someone noticed that I was not progressing socially.

The school guidance counselor wanted to find out what was going on and placed me in special education classes. During that time, the classes were labeled as "EMR," which meant the school had determined there was a need to place me in a specialized class. There was a stigma attached to being in that type of class. The same year during my ninth-grade year, I was in a terrible car accident with my family.

In Cleveland, Ohio there are expressways you can access to travel from one side of town to another. On this particular day, that's what we were doing. I sat in the front passenger seat beside my mother, who was driving. Two of my siblings sat in the back seat. All of a sudden, we were rear-ended by a car, which caused our car to start spinning around several times before it ended up against a fence on the shoulder. After the accident, two people came to the car and told my mother to turn off the car.

I don't remember seeing the people leave the scene of the accident in a car. We were all very shaken up after the accident. Most of us had minor injuries, except my brother who had a broken leg. When the ambulance arrived, they took my mother and my siblings to the hospital. I was left behind because they said it was not enough room in the ambulance and that another ambulance would be coming. It was traumatizing to be left at the scene of an accident as a child by myself.

The other ambulance did not come, but God sent a couple who transported me to the hospital. The accident report stated that when the other vehicle hit our car it was traveling seventy miles per hour upon impact. I know it is a miracle that God saved us from a tragedy. For years, I was traumatized by that event, mostly for being left at the scene of the accident.

During my tenth-grade year, I asked my parents to advocate for me so I could get out of special education classes and back into regular classes. I had goals to attend engineering school after graduation; but when I was in special education classes, they did not offer the math classes required for engineering school. I didn't understand why I was placed in a special education class, especially since I had no problems with academics.

Therefore, I hope this book will help parents who have children with special needs to advocate for proper evaluations before their children are placed in special needs/special education classes. I did graduate from high school, but I wanted so much to be in regular classes. At that point in my life, I was stigmatized with the label of being a student that was in special education classes.

I wanted to be an engineer, so I attended some classes at a junior college that I thought would help me in this process. It was overwhelming because my high school math classes did not prepare me for the math formulas in college. I was frustrated with school, the process, being labeled and because grade school did not properly prepare me for the future that I dreamed of for my life.

I transferred all my credits to a four-year college and changed my major to social work. I chose that major because I like to help people, so earning that degree would be a good fit for my life. I did not struggle in college with all my academics. Social skills were my biggest struggle in college. When I checked into my dorm room, I did not leave the room much, which caused people to knock on the door to check on me. Even in college, I remained withdrawn from people most of the time.

I had a hard time making friends and connecting with people. I kept to myself to try to protect myself from people. Me and my father were very close. He called me a few weeks before my college graduation. He said, "I am proud of you and I am looking forward to your graduation."

My father was very excited for me. He was the person who encouraged me to get through the growing pains of life. He helped me get through the low self-esteem issues and consistently assured me that I was going to be alright. Then I received a telephone call that my father was at home when he suddenly passed away from a heart attack.

My father's death not only shocked me, but it devastated me. I was hurt that he was gone. Since his passing, I have sought someone who could be a father figure to me, but that has not happened yet. At this time, I choose to believe that everything happens in God's timing.

When my father passed in March of 1989, he had been married to my mother for about thirty-five years. At the time of his passing, it seemed like life was just getting good for me and I wanted to share my joy with my father.

Me and my fiancé at the time were planning to get married in April of 1989. My father was going to officiate our wedding, which was another reason why his death devastated me.

CHAPTER
2
Love
and
Marriage

I believe it is important to include family in the important milestones of my life. It is important for family to work together.

Watching my parents over the years inspired me to get married. They worked so well together. They had a music ministry of their own and were great parents to seven children. Along with my parents being my inspiration, I chose to be married because I wanted to love someone and I wanted to be loved.

I believe marriage is a beautiful design by God. Our marriage started out good. We worked well together as a family unit. We operated like a team. I enjoyed having a family of my own to lead. I enjoyed family vacations and spending quality time together. It was so beautiful to me when we had the opportunity to sit down and enjoy meals together. It was also enjoyable to attend church together as a family.

We were blessed with the opportunity to nurture two children who live a good life. They are great children who did not get into trouble.

I had always been a family person, so I was used to having my family. Holiday dinners with family were always special for me. In our neighborhood, we placed special emphasis on cooking good food and enjoying a well-prepared meal with family. My wife and I often enjoyed family dinner and good conversation with our children.

"I still believe

marriage is

a beautiful design

by God."

CHAPTER

3

Diagnosis

My wife helped on my journey by advocating for me to seek help. I commend her for having the strength to stay with me for all the years she was with me. We invested in our marriage for years by going to counseling. As I continued going to counseling, things seemed to get worse. I became very depressed at times and I was frustrated. It seemed that the therapist could not find out what was going on with me.

My wife did research on the computer by typing in my symptoms. We found out that it was Autism Spectrum Disorder. The therapist that I was going to for help said I was a drain to their agency and that I was suffering from depression. I initially thought I was getting the help that I needed, but I was misdiagnosed again. Then, the therapist took me to court about a dispute. I was very disappointed with the whole situation.

It was so hurtful that it caused me to shut down again. I stopped going to therapy for several years. I prayed that God would send me to the right therapist to receive the help that I needed. Finally, in 2019 God led me to a facility in Valparaiso, Indiana that focused on family counseling. My new therapist provided me a proper diagnosis and the help that I needed. The diagnosis was Adult Autism Spectrum Disorder.

After the diagnosis, I participated in a research program at a hospital in Chicago, Illinois for one year. Once I arrived at the facility, I went for labs and completed a physical on a monthly basis. The program monitored the side effects of a new medicine, which was designed to improve the quality of life for people who were diagnosed with autism as adults. The purpose of the labs and the physicals was to monitor me physically and mentally to determine if there were any negative side effects.

Prior to the diagnosis, we struggled for years because we did not know what was going wrong with me. My wife often asked me, "What's wrong?" I would often reply, "I am okay." My other response was usually, "There is nothing wrong." I should have shared more with my wife so we could have worked through some of the issues together. As an adult, I've read that autism can usually be discovered in early childhood.

Therefore, it's quite possible that I had autism when I was a child, but was misdiagnosed. As a result, the frustration associated with the misdiagnosis caused a heavy burden on our marriage. When I reflect on the year 1989, it was a combination of an emotional rollercoaster and grief. In some ways, I kept the grief to myself after I attended a couple of sessions to help me with processing grief. I attended those few sessions because I did not want grief to overwhelm our marriage.

It was a lot to process because there were many different experiences rapidly occurring back-to-back. I really missed my father during my college graduation and our wedding. My father was also preparing me for ministry after I was licensed as a minister in 1988. In some ways, I did not really get over the grief; I just kept moving forward.

I tried my best to be a great new husband. I just went through the steps without processing the grief. It has been said that people with autism have deficits that don't allow proper processing of life events. That was my experience as it relates to the multiple levels of trauma surrounding the beginning of our marriage.

It felt like an unknown enemy was working against me; however, I didn't know at the time that the "unknown enemy" was actually autism. The main challenge was the fact that I could not help my wife and children emotionally.

I was able to work and be a great provider, but I did not have the capacity to properly show affection to my wife and children. Prior to marriage, I did inform my wife that I was sexually abused as a child. I also shared that I was working through some challenges. Not only did we agree to work through those challenges, but we also discussed working together to get through the issues that happened to us before we got married. Somehow along the way, we both grew tired and frustrated about what was going on in the marriage. There was a breakdown in our line of communication and we became two unhappy people.

The trauma from the car accident showed up in my marriage. When my wife and children left the house perhaps to go to the mall, it resembled abandonment to me. I did share the story about the accident with my wife. I also explained why being left alone felt like abandonment.

We were married for thirty-one years; however, I believe autism caused the breakdown of our marriage, which resulted in divorce. The journey to an autism diagnosis had a devastating effect on our marriage. The divorce was a difficult decision, but it was also a mutual agreement between me and my wife.

When the divorce was finalized in May 2020, I did not take any time off work to go through the grieving process. Once again, I just kept working because I did not know how to get through the grief. However, I experienced sickness for about three months after receiving the divorce decree. I believe it was the emotional pain of the divorce that caused physical pain in my body. There were days that I did not think I would make it; however, in the process I learned that with God, all things are possible. I learned how to be refreshed by God on a consistent basis.

I was at home when the divorce decree came in the mail. The separation process was underway because we had been spending so much time away from each other. I've often wondered, "How do you sever a relationship when someone has been with you for more than thirty years?" It was not an easy experience for me. I did grieve heavily after I moved out the house. It seemed like I was physically sick each day, but I knew I had to focus more on God and what He wanted me to do with the rest of my life.

All the frustration of not knowing what was wrong with me took its toll on our marriage of thirty-one years. Nevertheless, I learned a lot about myself in those thirty-one years. When I experienced the divorce, I had to face my biggest fears. I feared not knowing how to do things alone. I also feared not knowing how to take care of myself without the additional support.

I had so many questions like: *"How would I survive being by myself without my family? Would people try to take advantage of me? How would I learn to speak up for myself?"*

When my wife and I mutually agreed to end our marriage after thirty-one years, that left a big hole in my emotions. At that point, I felt like a complete failure in life and that I could not do anything right. After the autism diagnosis in 2019 followed by the divorce in May 2020, life was very difficult because of all the years that we had invested. It was a turning point in my life and I had to learn how to redefine my new life.

The divorce was painful, but I realized the importance of learning how to move forward from the painful struggles in life. It was also scary because I was older and I was alone. I often wondered, "What is going to happen to me now?"

I did ask, "God why?" I knew I could not dwell there, so I had to refocus my life to see what direction God wanted to take me next. I was able to refocus by choosing to reflect on the positive experiences in our marriage. Writing my book became a form of inspiration for me.

In reality, none of the things that I feared happened to me because God is faithful. God provided me with the tools needed to survive in the world without my family. I still attend talk therapy, which has really helped me. I've made a new commitment to God because everything was new to me. I have learned to pray and trust God for my protection. God has been faithful to help me get through each day victoriously.

Since the diagnosis, I have been working to get my life back on track. I became dedicated to the reality that God can bring you out of any situation. God has guided me to people who are prayerful and supportive.

Sometimes, I've felt angry with God because of all the hurt and pain I've been through. I've expressed anger through frustration. I did not want to harm anyone; therefore, I learned to live according to the Scripture that I read in Ephesians 4:26, "Be angry, yet do not sin."

Sometimes people express anger through different ways, such as road rage. As a son of God, I have a mindset that God will always bring me out of every challenge that I face in life. I developed this mindset while going through the process of divorce.

There were some positive things that God gave me and that is what I choose to focus on in my life. I reflected on how God carried me through at other phases of my life, doing so, helped me survive divorce. Now, I am in a place where I spend my days in prayer and fasting, seeking God for every step in my life. I stay positive and I stay focused.

**"There were days
that I did not think I would make it;
however,
in the process I learned that
with God,
all things are possible.
I learned how to be refreshed by God
on a consistent basis."**

CHAPTER
4
Renewed Mindset

D o not conform to the pattern of this world, but be transformed by the renewing of your mind. Then you will be able to test and approve what God's will is—his good, pleasing and perfect will. Romans 12:2 (NIV)

There was a time when I was unsure about where I was headed spiritually and emotionally. Then I chose to adapt to living a consecrated lifestyle. Each Saturday from midnight until about 4 p.m. I pray, fast, read Scriptures and leave my audio Bible on all night as I sleep.

Hearing the Word of God gives me strength. Knowing that God helps me on a continual basis has equipped me to overcome the challenges that I have faced. The Word of God literally became the strength that pulled me up out of the anger I had due to the divorce. I had to learn how to live according to the Scripture Ephesians 6:10, "Be strong in the Lord and in the power of His might."

I grasped the Word of God and literally believed what God said to be truth for my life. God helped me through divorce by covering me according to the promise of Ephesians 6:11, "Put on the whole armor of God, that you may be able to stand against the schemes of the devil."

I am hopeful today because I know that God gave me another chance by bringing restoration to my life. My faith has been restored. At one time, I was hopeless because I did not know what was going to happen or where I was going in my life. However, I often gain encouragement by listening to the testimonies of people who found hope after divorce.

Some of the people I heard about who became hopeless also became depressed and did not want to live. I thank God for giving me hope. I am thankful for the people who continuously pray for me.

I am thankful for each day because that means that I have been given another chance to rebuild my personal relationship with God. I had to really trust God to carry me and He continuously sustains me.

The trauma from the car accident resurfaced after the divorce. To get over the issue of abandonment, I intentionally schedule time to read, to pray, to watch T.V. and to go for drives to break up the monotony of being alone. The divorce was like a bee sting; but at some point, I had to pick up the pieces and move forward with my life. Focusing on the plans that God has for my life fuels me to keep moving forward.

There were once opposing thoughts that would tell me, "You're no good because you had a divorce and all the things you went through."

I had to choose to move forward and put all the problems in the hands of God. I choose not to worry and I choose not to live with anxiety. Instead, I trust God more.

I often turn to music for encouragement. I listen to music, mostly when I am driving. "There Will Be Glory After This" is a song that brings me hope. One time, I did ask, "God, why did I have to go through a divorce?" Now, I understand there is nothing too hard for God. I know God still wants the best out of me and the best for me in life.

I've read Romans 8:28 and it caused me to wonder, "How can divorce work together for my good?" I had to relax in God. I learned to trust God more. I learned to believe in God and build a stronger relationship with God than I had ever experienced in my life. I have a renewed perspective about my life. It is similar to spring—a season that represents something spiritual because it comes after cold days.

Once the weather warms up, the flowers grow and the grass is green. For me, there is deliverance in sharing my story through a book. I get to release the painful seasons of life to make room for something beautiful to grow in my life again.

Spring also represents the morning as in the dawning of a new day. It is a time for remembering what God did to sustain me in the past. I trust God for all the seasons of my life. I believe that anxiety can negatively affect health and that is why I intentionally release anxiety.

Doubt, fear, worry and anxiety can hinder and hurt a person. There are probably a lot of people facing challenges that resulted during the pandemic. I encourage everyone I can to trust God, even during challenging times. I trust God to give me a new beginning on a daily basis.

I thought about the children of Israel and how God delivered them out of all they went through. However, they complained in the wilderness on a consistent basis. I do not want to live a life of complaining to God. I have been blessed with the gift of time to reflect on the marriage. I've learned how to do some things for myself in those thirty-one years of marriage and our two years of friendship.

However, there were stages in the marriage when I was too co-dependent on my wife. Some of that was due to the autism. Since I've been living by myself, I am learning how to be more independent.

I have intentionally focused on maintaining a relationship with our children after divorce by sending messages consistently. I call to check on them. I send them cards and gifts on their birthdays as well as on special holidays. I did that while I was present in the household and I am intentional about keeping those traditions.

We talk and they spend time with me when their schedules are open. In the quiet moments of life, I still have dreams and goals for my future that include the opportunity to keep working with my music. My support system includes God, music and therapy.

I have been in churches where they've made it known in the African American community that if you went to therapy, then something was wrong with you. However, it has been helpful for me to have someone to listen who is equipped to provide help, support, information and tools for me to get through challenges in life. Yes, I do believe God heals; however, I also believe it is very important to have access to therapy for support. It is also important to allow your family access to your life because they can also help on your journey. My family members in Ohio have been very supportive and they call to check on me.

I believe if I would have known about the autism earlier, that would have been helpful. I was used to being around family because that was my comfort zone. I've doubted myself a lot and wondered, "How will I get through this life alone?"

I have gained self-confidence through my daily devotion time with God, reading Scripture, listening to gospel music and being around people at work who speak kind words of encouragement to me. The Word of God brings strength and healing to me. The gospel music also breaks yokes of bondage.

When I face challenges now, I think about some of the other things that God carried me through. I shift my focus to reading the Word of God and praying. I have learned that a renewed mindset leads to renewed strength.

"I am hopeful today because I know that God gave me another chance by bringing restoration to my life."

CHAPTER 5

On the Right Path

I was able to get on the right path in life by shifting from struggling, to living in my main strengths: grace, persistence, patience and compassion. Sometimes, listening to people share their stories can be very encouraging. Another one of my strengths is the ability to listen to people for the purpose of helping them through their problems. Now, I can perhaps help someone else who has experienced a divorce. It can be a very difficult experience. However, I can encourage someone to keep moving forward in life.

I relocated to another city after praying and seeking God for direction. I wanted to move somewhere that was safe. I was seeking a studio or one-bedroom apartment. When I applied for an apartment, the rental agent told me there were no openings. Then, the rental agent called me back and told me that there were two-bedroom apartments available on the first floor.

It is a community that provides a safe place. The ability to move was another indicator that I was on the right path. I have learned there are important steps to *grow through* what you go through in life. First, it is important to ask God for direction. Then, move in the direction where God is leading you. I sought a quiet place to live so that I could clearly hear the direction that God has for me. Sometimes, even if a space does not look like the one you want, it can still work together for your good. Sometimes, when we ask God for something, we are asking too small.

The two-bedroom apartment was the greater that God wanted me to have because He knows what's going to happen during every stage of my life. I went back to look at the two-bedroom apartment because I want all of what God wants for me. The second bedroom will be used as a studio for my music. The experience reminded me of the song, "What God has for me is for me."

I also believe it is important to write the vision and make it plain. Therefore, I put up a chart in my room which outlines my vision for my life. I decided to write my life goals' list and what I wanted to do next with my life. It included writing a book and earning a master's degree. I have learned that it is important to invite God into your goals and to be specific.

Writing goals and putting those goals in a place where I can actually see on a daily basis helps me to remain focused. I know that I have purpose, but my goals were not coming together the way I wanted them to in the past. I encourage everyone to write goals and a clear vision.

Just because you've experienced something negative like a divorce does not mean your life is over. As long as you are breathing, there is purpose for your life. I have learned that I am capable of doing good because God created me to do good.

I have learned that I do have good qualities because of who God created me to be. I am a faithful, praying man because God keeps me in perfect peace. I am dedicated to renewing my mind on a consistent basis. I am a man of great devotion to God and I am consistently doing the inside work.

After the research program, I reflected on my life and decided to continue with talk therapy because I have experienced great results. I also found a supportive therapist in Gary, Indiana. The therapist that I go to now really focuses on the healing practices of God and talk therapy. I am so thankful that I started and continued the process of talk therapy.

"I want to be remembered for achieving success after an adult autism diagnosis."

CHAPTER
6
Faith
Forward

I am able to faith forward in life today because I have learned that I have the right to choose to focus more on God than on the diagnosis and past pain. Faith forward is the ability to view life according to my faith and not according to the challenges in life. Therefore, I encourage people to speak well about their life instead of believing the negative report of the enemy. I was able to defeat feelings of doubt by speaking words of faith. These are some of the words of encouragement that I speak to cancel doubt:

- I am going to make it today.

- Today is going to be a good day.

- I will get through this today.

- I am hopeful.

- I choose to focus more on God than on the diagnosis and past pain.

As I write this book, I am one assignment away from finishing my first class in my graduate program. It is a graduate-level writing class. During a rough time in life, God has favored me and I am thankful for the progress that I have made in school. God has shown me that there is a reward in obedience.

I was online one day and a college sent me information to my email. I enrolled in college online where I was allowed to take one class at a time. The fact that I could take one class at a time was a perfect fit for my life and my learning style. I took orientation and it was challenging, so I applied again in January 2021. My class began February 9, 2021. Even with all the struggles of the year 2020, I continued walking in the favor of God. I feel like God has rehabbed my life. It is a good kind of life. I anticipate graduating as a member of the class of 2023.

Attending college online as an older student has been challenging, especially with all of the writing requirements. It was a fear of the unknown; however, I am consistently growing in confidence. When I passed one class, that gave me the courage to keep going, knowing that I can keep passing classes. I believe God is a miracle worker. I also believe that one act of courage begets more courage.

The time that we're living in with societal changes and covid-19, it has caused a lot of people to face plenty of challenges. I have processed all the challenges by believing God and believing in what God created me to do on earth. I pray to God to say, "Thank you." I don't pray with a long list of things I want; instead, I pray to God with a heart of gratitude. I want to be remembered for achieving success after an adult autism diagnosis.

I believe there is a misconception that people with autism can't do anything or be successful in life. What God has allowed me to achieve in life thus far is worthy of celebrating. I want to be remembered for proving the status quo to be wrong. I also want to be remembered for staying focused, setting and achieving all my goals. I am dedicated to taking the limits off God in my life by living a life where God is not placed inside of a box. I am also dedicated to living a life that God has already prepared for greatness. God is so powerful and awesome.

At certain times, I've tried to figure out how God would bring me out of certain situations. Even when I did not know how God would work things out, every situation still worked together for my good. I choose to focus on the favor of God. It is new to me and it is good. Even after I experienced depression and anger, I consistently choose to continue to trust God. Life is good for me now.

I celebrate my wins by praising God. I don't have many friends, so I talk to my family and they encourage me to keep going. I am dedicated to focusing more on pushing past fear. I have learned to trust God more now than ever before. When I step up to one thing, I see God work. Then, I go to a higher step in life. I see God work. Then, I go to another step. My life thus far has been a process of taking one step after another while trusting God with each step. I have learned to be more courageous.

I am excited about my life right now. I am thankful to be alive and living in good health. I get to live with the understanding that God is with me. I get to live with the understanding that God is helping me as I continue to work and move forward in life. The reason that I chose the title for this book is because of my occupation as a commercial driver.

Some of the same concepts that I've learned as a commercial driver, can also be associated with life. For example, there is a process called the Pre-Trip Inspection, which is under federal law. The driver must inspect the vehicle for defects prior to driving. If you don't complete the pre-trip inspection properly and something happens such as an accident, then you would be considered liable for the accident. However, with the proper Pre-Trip Inspection, you are destined to have a great experience on the road.

The Pre-Trip Inspection is like life because God has completed a pre-trip of our lives to ensure that we have a great experience on the road called life. The Bible also tells us in Ephesians 1:11 that we were predestined before we were born. God already knew who we would be, how we would look and our personality.

The Scripture in Luke 12:7 even tells us that God knows how many hairs we have on our head. I believe I am still standing today because God is so involved in the details of my life.

Just like it is important to conduct a Pre-Trip Inspection as a professional driver, it is important to invest time in reflection so you can thrive in life. I have invested the time to reflect on my life, decisions that I have made, lessons from the past and the possibilities in my future. I have made the decision to totally trust God with my life.

CHAPTER
7

Resources

I want to share what I have learned about Autism Spectrum Disorder. I believe it is important for people to be informed about what happens with autism so that children can receive the help they need at an early age in life. The National Institute of Mental Health and Neurosciences has identified Autism Spectrum Disorder (ASD) as a developmental disorder that affects communication and behavior.

Although autism can be diagnosed at any age, it is said to be a "developmental disorder" because symptoms generally appear in children during the first two years of life. Autism is known as a "spectrum" disorder because there is wide variation in the type and severity of symptoms people experience. ASD occurs in all ethnic, racial, and economic groups. Although ASD can be a lifelong disorder, treatments and services can improve a person's symptoms as well as their ability to function.

The American Academy of Pediatrics recommends that all children be screened for autism. All caregivers should talk to their doctor about ASD screening or evaluation.

Signs and Symptoms of ASD:

People with ASD may have difficulty with social communication and interaction, restricted interests and repetitive behaviors. The list below gives some examples of the types of behaviors that are seen in people diagnosed with ASD. Not all people with ASD will show all behaviors, but most will show several.

Social communication / interaction behaviors may include:

- Making little or inconsistent eye contact
- Tending not to look at or listen to people

- Rarely sharing enjoyment of objects or activities by pointing or showing things to others

- Failing to, or being slow to, respond to someone calling their name or to other verbal attempts to gain attention

- Having difficulties with the back and forth of conversation

- Often talking at length about a favorite subject without noticing that others are not interested or without giving others a chance to respond

- Having facial expressions, movements, and gestures that do not match what is being said

- Having an unusual tone of voice that may sound flat, sing-song or robot-like

- Having trouble understanding another person's point of view or being unable to predict or understand other people's actions

Restrictive/repetitive behaviors may include:

- Repeating certain behaviors or having unusual behaviors

- Repeating words or phrases, a behavior called *echolalia*

- Having a lasting, intense interest in certain topics, such as numbers, details or facts

- Having overly focused interests, such as with moving objects or parts of objects

- Getting upset by slight changes in a routine

- Being more or less sensitive than other people to sensory input, such as light, noise, clothing or temperature

People with ASD may also experience sleep problems and irritability. Although people with ASD experience many challenges, they may also have many strengths, including:

- Being able to learn things in detail and remember information

I have also learned that autism can happen due to low birth weight. Children who are born underweight may have some developmental challenges. I had a very low birth weight and I was considered premature because I was born early. It can sometimes be detected when children go to the doctor for their wellness check-ups at the early stage of life.

Early diagnosis and treatment can lead to a better quality of life. That is the key to making progress in life. In my case, none of the doctors detected this when I went for my wellness checks.

My plan of care after diagnosis:

1. I continue to attend talk therapy.

2. My therapist continues to monitor my progress in talk therapy.

3. I grew in my ability to believe God as I attended therapy.

4. The greatest benefits of therapy for me was knowing that the therapist was supportive.

5. When I had ideas and goals to accomplish things in life, the therapist was very encouraging.

6. I had never been a person to set goals in life, but the therapist emphasized the importance of setting goals.

7. The therapist asked me about my goals for the next two weeks.

8. I have accountability check-ins with the therapist.

9. I continue to have new dreams at every stage in my life.

10. God is constantly encouraging me to keep dreaming. As long as God gives me dreams, I am dedicated to living my dreams.

There are valuable ways to help someone who has been diagnosed with autism. Listed below are three ways to immediately help someone diagnosed with autism:

1. See the human.

2. See the strengths.

3. Discover the areas of genius.

I encourage you to invest the time to see the strengths after your spouse, family member, friend or child has been diagnosed with autism. In reality, a person who has been diagnosed with autism is still a human with areas of genius who can bring joy to your life.

About the Author

Mr. Thomas Burton

Through faith and perseverance, Mr. Thomas Burton has defied the odds by living a productive life despite an autism diagnosis. After experiencing sixty years of life filled with unanswered questions and a misdiagnosis, he is now clear on his purpose. He has discovered the resilience to get his life on the right track. With higher education being one of his life goals, he is currently pursuing a master's degree in ministry.

He wrote *Driving Through Life* at 63 years old to offer hope and to share valuable life lessons. With a compassionate heart for people, he is on a mission to help people heal by authentically sharing his story. Mr. Burton continues his journey through life with a commitment to consistent personal and professional development.

HOPE

"I hope this book will help parents who have children with special needs, to advocate for proper evaluations before their children are placed in special needs/special education classes."

HOPE

"Early diagnosis and treatment can lead to a better quality of life."

HOW TO HELP

Driving Through Life What was I Thinking?

SEE
THE
HUMAN.

HOW TO HELP

SEE THE STRENGTHS.

HOW TO HELP

DISCOVER THE AREAS OF GENIUS.

ENCOURAGEMENT

TODAY IS GOING TO BE A GOOD DAY.

ENCOURAGEMENT

I AM GOING TO MAKE IT TODAY.

ENCOURAGEMENT

I AM HOPEFUL.

ENCOURAGEMENT

I WILL GET THROUGH THIS TODAY.

ENCOURAGEMENT

"What God has allowed me to achieve in life thus far is worthy of celebrating."

ENCOURAGEMENT

I

AM

FOCUSED.

ENCOURAGEMENT

I ACHIEVE MY GOALS.

ENCOURAGEMENT

I AM MORE THAN A DIAGNOSIS.

ENCOURAGEMENT

I

AM

SAFE.

www.ingramcontent.com/pod-product-compliance
Lightning Source LLC
Chambersburg PA
CBHW071236090426
42736CB00014B/3103